The story of shweshwe

MADE IN SOUTH AFRICA

Lynn Barnes

Words that are in bold, like **this**, are explained in the Word help, on the page and at the end of the book.

The *Made in South Africa* series is published by
Awareness Publishing Group (Pty) Ltd.
Copyright © 2019

Awareness Publishing (SA) (Pty) Ltd
www.awareness.co.za
info@awareness.co.za
+27 (0)86 110 1491
www.facebook.com/AwarenessPublishing

All rights reserved. No part of this publication may be reproduced in any form without written permission from the publisher, except by a reviewer.

First edition 2019

The story of shweshwe by Lynn Barnes
ISBN 978-1-77008-990-7

Summary: A simple introduction to shweshwe, including some details of its history in South Africa, and how it is made.

Book design: Richard Keenan-Smith and Elizabeth Barnard

Editorial credits: Managing editor: Monique le Riché; Copy editor: Danya Ristić-Schacherl; Picture editors: Anne Laing and Lawrence Frank

Picture credits: Cover © Da Gama Textiles; cover (background) © Christopher / Fotolia; cover (flag) © Kurt / Dreamstime; endpapers © Da Gama Textiles; p4 © Carina Beyer / Iziko Museums of South Africa; p6 (top) © Christopher / Fotolia; p6 (bottom) © Anna Velichkovsky / Fotolia; p8 © AAI FotoStock SA / Alamy / Art Collection 3; p10 © Iziko Museums of Cape Town / Africa Media Online; p12 © casadaphoto / Depositphotos; p13 © rinderart / Depositphotos; p14 © Da Gama Textiles; p15 © Bianca Keenan-Smith; p16 © Da Gama Textiles; p18 (both) © Nicholas Schlemmer; p20 (both) © Luca Vincenzo; p21 © Nicholas Schlemmer; p22 © Da Gama Textiles; p24 © Da Gama Textiles; p26 © Da Gama Textiles; p28 © Scott Wilson; p30 © Chell Hill / Wikipedia; p32 (left) © Da Gama Textiles; p32 (middle) © Chameleon Studios / JenniDezigns – https://jennidezigns.clothing/; p32 (right) © Da Gama Textiles; p34 (both) © Da Gama Textiles; p36 © Blue Square Quilting; p38 © Da Gama Textiles; p40 © nancyzieman.com; p40 (inset) © Carina Beyer / Iziko Museums of South Africa

The author would like to thank Helen Bester of Da Gama Textiles for reviewing the manuscript and providing additional information and photographs.

1 3 5 7 9 0 8 6 4 2

Contents

Beautiful cloth 5
Brought to South Africa by traders 7
How did the cloth get its name? 9
Making shweshwe cloth 11
Shweshwe is made from cotton 13
Making cloth 15
Getting the colours 17
Making the patterns 19
Patterns and pictures 21
Stiff with starch 23
Brand names 25
Real shweshwe cloth 27
Look for the real thing 29
South Africans love shweshwe 31
More new colours 33
The world of fashion 35
Across the world 37
Word help 39

A beautiful dress made from shweshwe.

Beautiful cloth

Shweshwe (we say: shway-shway) is a type of cloth that many people in South Africa like to wear. It is made from cotton.

A rainbow has seven colours.

red   orange   yellow   green   blue   indigo   violet

Indigo is one of the colours of the rainbow.

Brought to South Africa by traders

Many years ago traders brought a type of cloth to South Africa. It was called indigo cloth because it was a very dark blue like the indigo colour in a rainbow.

Indigo is a very dark blue.

King Moshweshwe.

How did the cloth get its name?

Some people say that the name comes from King Moshweshwe (we say: Mo-shway-shway). In the 1840s **missionaries** came to Africa and gave some indigo cloth to the king as a gift. Then, people called the cloth shweshwe, after the king.

> **Word help**
>
> **missionaries:** people who go to other countries to teach about Christianity

Other people say it is called shweshwe because of the swishing sound it makes when someone who is wearing it moves: shwe – shwe.

Ships brought indigo cloth from Europe to South Africa.

Making shweshwe cloth

For many years the cloth was brought to South Africa from Europe on ships. But since 1982 shweshwe cloth has been made in South Africa by a company called Da Gama Textiles at a factory in Eastern Cape.

Machines collecting the cotton balls from the plants in a cotton field.

Shweshwe is made from cotton

Cotton grows on plants in a field. Machines pick the fluffy white cotton balls. Then the cotton goes on trucks to a factory.

A fluffy cotton ball growing on a cotton plant.

A factory worker checking the calico cloth.

Making cloth

At the factory, machines clean the cotton and make it into long, thin threads. Then machines weave the threads under and over each other to make a plain white or cream-coloured cloth. This cloth is called calico.

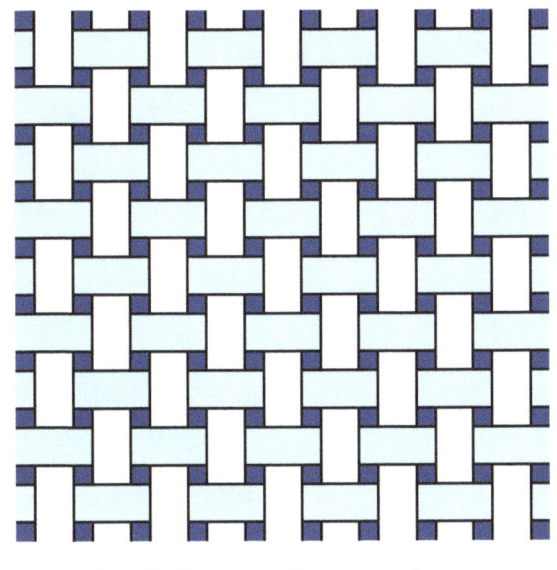

A picture of weaving.

A machine that uses dyes to colour cloth. You can see the cream calico going in at the bottom and the same piece of cloth now coloured indigo at the top.

Getting the colours

Dyes are used to make the cloth one colour all over. At first, shweshwe cloth was made only in indigo, but later it was made in several different colours. The most popular colours were indigo, brown and red.

> **Word help**
>
> **dyes:** coloured liquids used to change the colour of something, such as a piece of cloth

A roller with a pattern of tiny holes in it.

Pieces of shweshwe showing the white patterns made by the acid on the coloured cloth.

Making the patterns

The plain-coloured cloth then goes into a machine and moves under a roller that has patterns of little holes cut into it.

A weak **acid** is passed through the roller. The acid can only touch the cloth in the places where there are holes in the roller. Where it touches the cloth it takes out the colour. This leaves white patterns on the coloured cloth.

Different rollers are used to make different patterns.

> **Word help**
> **acid:** a liquid that can take the colour out of cloth

Left: Shweshwe panels. The dotted white lines show where to cut the cloth. Right: Shweshwe panels that have been cut out and sewn together to make a skirt.

Patterns and pictures

Shweshwe comes in many different patterns. Some shweshwe has the same pattern all over. Some is made with sections, called panels. The panels can be cut out and sewn together to make clothes, such as skirts. Sometimes the panels have pictures of important people on them.

Shweshwe panels with pictures of Nelson Mandela on them.

This machine puts starch onto the cloth.

Stiff with starch

New shweshwe cloth is soaked with **starch** to protect it. This makes the cloth very stiff. Washing the cloth takes out the starch and leaves the cloth soft and smooth.

> **Word help**
> **starch:** a substance that makes cloth stiff

THREE CATS is the brand name that the Da Gama company puts on its shweshwe cloth.

Brand names

A brand name is a special name that a company gives to things that it makes or sells. Coca-Cola and Colgate are examples of brand names. The Da Gama company uses the brand name THREE CATS for shweshwe cloth. This name is printed on the back of the cloth. If the cloth does not have this brand name on the back, it may not be real shweshwe.

Real shweshwe is made only in South Africa.

Real shweshwe cloth

Other countries, such as China, have tried to produce a similar type of shweshwe cloth. It is cheaper but it is not the real thing. Real shweshwe is made in South Africa.

A woman smelling cloth to see if it is real shweshwe.

Look for the real thing

People can tell real shweshwe by the feel, the smell, the sound and even the taste of the cloth. They can also tell by looking for the brand name on the back of the cloth.

Indigo shweshwe is used to make part of the traditional dress of these Xhosa women.

South Africans love shweshwe

Shweshwe has always been popular in South Africa. People use it to make dresses, aprons and head scarves.

African people like to wear shweshwe for special occasions such as weddings.

Nowadays, shweshwe is available in lots of bright colours.

More new colours

Now shweshwe cloth is made in even more colours. It is available in bright colours such as pink, orange and turquoise. These colours are often used for making children's clothes.

Turquoise is a greenish-blue colour.

Models wearing dresses made with shweshwe cloth.

The world of fashion

In the last few years South African designers have begun using shweshwe in their fashion clothes. This has made shweshwe more popular than ever.

Shweshwe cloth can be used for making patchwork quilts.

Across the world

Nowadays people everywhere are interested in shweshwe. Countries all over the world buy shweshwe from South Africa. Many people like to use shweshwe to make **patchwork quilts**.

> **Word help**
>
> **patchwork quilts:** bed covers made by sewing together small pieces of cloth; the pieces are often different colours and are arranged to make a pattern

An outfit made of shweshwe with panels in the skirt.

Word help

acid: a liquid that can take the colour out of cloth

dyes: coloured liquids used to change the colour of something, such as a piece of cloth

missionaries: people who go to other countries to teach about Christianity

patchwork quilts: bed covers made by sewing together small pieces of cloth; the pieces are often different colours and are arranged to make a pattern

starch: a substance that makes cloth stiff

A handbag made from shweshwe cloth.
Inset: People even use shweshwe to make shoes.

www.ingramcontent.com/pod-product-compliance
Lightning Source LLC
Chambersburg PA
CBHW051259110526
44589CB00025B/2884